How do I get to Heaven? offers a clear and compelling presentation of the Gospel that a child can understand. Repentance, faith, regeneration, justification, adoption, and even glorification are all explained in simple language. Parents and grandparents will enjoy reading this with young children, and those who hear will be blessed as they grasp the greatest good news this world has ever heard.

Colin S. Smith
Senior Pastor, The Orchard
Founder and Bible Teacher, Open the Bible

Having often preached on Revelation 21:1-4 at funerals, I confess I was so moved I found myself in tears as I read the opening pages of this children's book. It is just incredibly moving and a quite wonderful resource to help us give real hope to children ... and indeed adults.

Rico Tice
Author and Founder, Christianity Explored Ministries

This book belongs to:

....

10 9 8 7 6 5 4 3 2 1

Copyright © 2024 Nancy Gorrell
Paperback ISBN: 978-1-5271-1066-3

Published by Christian Focus Publications,
Geanies House, Fearn, Tain, Ross-shire,
IV20 1TW, Scotland, U.K.
www.christianfocus.com;
email: info@christianfocus.com

Cover designer: Martyn Smith
Cover and internal illustrations by Martyn Smith
Printed and bound in China

How Do I Get to Heaven?

Questions and Answers about
Life and Death

Nancy Gorrell

Illustrated by Martyn Smith

There is a place that you can go where it will never be bedtime.
You will never be tired or sleepy and there is never any night there.
The sky is always bright with beautiful light.
That means there is never any darkness to be afraid of
and there will never be any more bad dreams!

There is a place that you can go where no one is ever sick.
There are no doctor's offices or hospitals –
no one there gets a runny nose or earache or an upset tummy.
There aren't even any scraped knees and there's no tangled hair!

Everyone can run and jump and dance.
Every eye can see the bright beauty;
every ear can hear the sweet songs.

There will be no more night.
(Revelation 22:5)

There will be no more death or
mourning or crying or pain.
(Revelation 21:4)

There is a place that you can go to where no one ever sins.
Everyone is always perfectly good all of the time.
All the people there are friends.
There is no fighting or crying or hurt feelings.

This place is more beautiful and amazing than you could ever imagine.

Think of glorious angels, mighty heroes, pretty music and happy friends.
All these things are there and much, much more!
But even these marvellous things are not the best parts about it.
Do you think this place sounds like make-believe? It's not!
The Bible says that this wonderful place is called heaven.

The Holy City... shone with the glory of God,
and its brilliance was like that of a very precious jewel.
(Revelation 21:10–11)

Heaven is the best place ever because God made it to be
a perfect and excellent place of blessing for his children.
It is a splendid and holy place because God is there.
God the Father, Jesus and the Holy Spirit make heaven beautiful and bright.
It is filled with love, light and joy. All the people who are there
praise and bless Jesus for saving them. They love God and they love each other.
There is no place happier than heaven. There is no place more full of love.

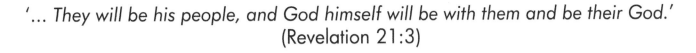

'... They will be his people, and God himself will be with them and be their God.'
(Revelation 21:3)

Does heaven seem very far away to you?
You know, I have told you that this is a place where you can go.
How do you get to heaven?
Do you drive in the car? Maybe you can take a bus?
Can you swim there? I know! You use a ladder, don't you?
"No, No!" you answer. Jesus is the one who takes you to heaven.

'... what must I do to be saved?'
(Acts 16:30)

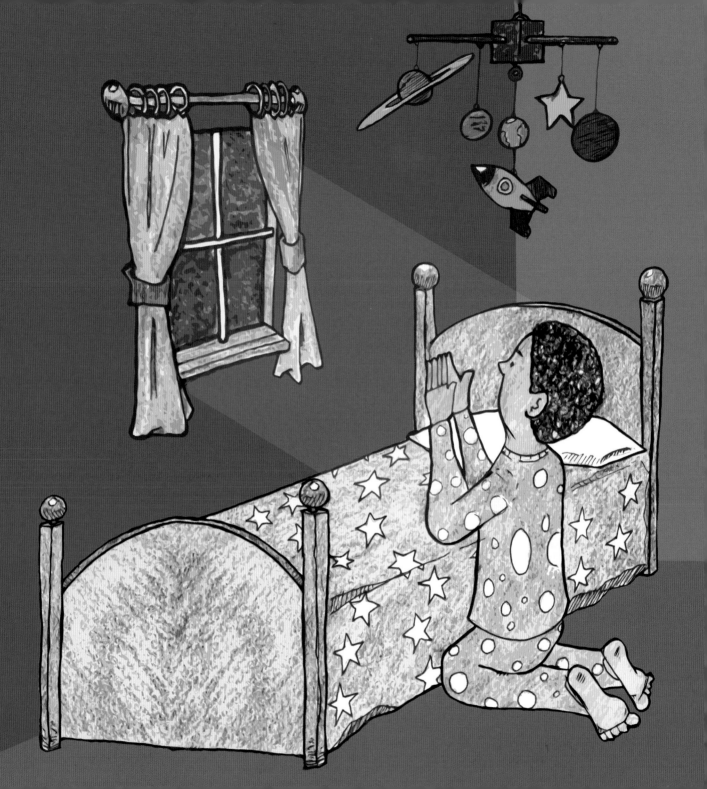

Jesus came to earth to live and die for his people.
He obeyed for them because he knew they couldn't, and
he died for them so that they wouldn't be punished for their sins.
All the little children who love and trust Jesus go to heaven.
God brings all of his people, whom he loves very dearly,
to come to be with him there.

"I love and trust Jesus!" you say.
"I've asked him to forgive my sins.
When can I go up? Can I go up now?"

Jesus is the one who decides when you go
and you have to wait for him to call you.
Then he'll send angels to take you there.

You'll be very happy, but you have to wait for Jesus.

'... I desire to depart and be with Christ, which is better by far ...'
(Philippians 1:23)

Some people do go up to heaven when they are young and some people get to go when they're very little babies, but most people are old before they go to heaven. Jesus has much for them to do here first. Then, at the right time, their bodies die and their spirits – the part that lasts forever – go up to be with Jesus.

The Bible calls dying "falling asleep". The outside part of you, the part you can touch, goes quietly to sleep, while your soul goes up to God. Your body rests in the ground until the day that Jesus comes back. But your soul is happy in heaven while your body is sleeping. On the day that Jesus comes back, he will call your body up out of the ground and he will reunite it with your spirit.
This is called a resurrection.
But your body will be better! Jesus will fix it so that it is perfect!
No more stubbed toes, bruises or tummy aches.

We believe that God will bring with Jesus those who have fallen asleep in him.
(1 Thessalonians 4:14)

God's Bible does say that going to heaven is a wonderful thing.
Jesus wants his people there. He loves them so much that
he prays to his Father for them to come up to be with him.
So why are people sad when the ones they love get to go there?
Because sometimes it's hard to say goodbye.
Did you ever cry when you had to leave your granny's house?

But you're very happy when you get to see her again, aren't you?

Just think, in heaven, you'll never have to say goodbye again!
Just one happy "hello" over and over again!
With the best and the happiest "hello" to Jesus who loved you the most!

You will never be happier than you will be in heaven.
You will be happy because God is there and
God is the one who makes heaven perfect.
This God, who makes heaven perfect, loves children just like you!
You can go to heaven because he invites you to come!
He sent his only son, Jesus, to do everything that
needed to be done so that you could go there.
And Jesus is already there now!
He is praying for his people and waiting happily for them.
He is very excited about welcoming his special
ones to their glorious home with God!

Love Jesus.
Sing songs to him because he loved you first.
Trust him with all your heart, and some day
you will be able to see Jesus with your very own eyes.
You will be able to look at him, hug him, thank him
and tell him that you love him.
That will be the best part about heaven.
How happy you will be!

HALLELUJAH

'Father, I want those you have given me to be with me where I am,
and to see my glory ...'
(John 17:24)

God's special book, the Bible, is full of very important lessons for you.
Did you know that every truth in God's Bible should help you
to learn about a very wonderful person?
That person is the Lord and Savior, Jesus Christ.
Jesus Christ is God's Son. He always lived with God in heaven,
even before anything you see was made!
That he is a son does not mean that he was ever a little baby in heaven or
even that God made him one day before God made anything else.

*The Father has sent his Son to be the
Savior of the world.*
(1 John 4:14)

WHAT A
BEAUTIFUL
MAN.

When you go to see your grandma, does she squeeze your cheeks and say,
"Ooo, you look just like your daddy"?
Maybe you do look like your dad. Maybe some day
you will look and act like your father does now.
Jesus is exactly like God, his Father. He is powerful like God;
he has always lived, just like his Father has.
All the things that make God his Father special, make Jesus special too!
They are the same, and yet they are two different persons.
The Holy Spirit is also the same as them but different.
Together all three are called the trinity.

'For the Father loves the Son and shows him all he does.'
(John 5:20)

Before God ever made the world, he gave his only Son, Jesus, a wonderful gift.
He gave Jesus a special group of people that he would create
to be Jesus' very own.

Jesus loves his people very much, so he wants
them to come to heaven to be with him.

But he knew that his people did not love him.
They did wrong things and could not come to God's perfect home, heaven.
So Jesus had to do a very hard job.

'Father, I want those you have given me to be with me where I am, and to see my glory ...'
(John 17:24)

'They were yours; you gave them to me ...'
(John 17:6)

Jesus had to be born on earth as
a baby, just as you were born!

This is called the incarnation.
God's Son took a body
and became a real human being,
a real baby boy.

Then Jesus had to live a perfect life.
He never stole anything or was
unhappy with the things he had,
even though he was very
poor while he lived on the earth.

He never beat up his little brothers
and sisters, or lied, or said unkind words,
or even thought bad things!

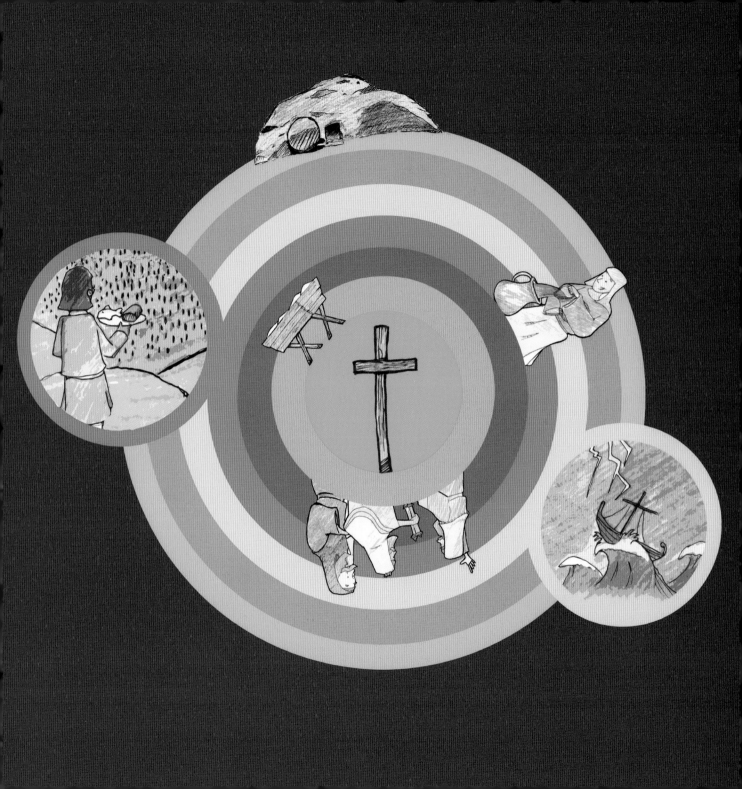

When Jesus became a grown-up man, he worked
very hard to teach people about God.
Sometimes people hated him or hurt him or made him sad, but he did not quit.
Then Jesus had to die a very terrible and painful death on the cross.

This is called the crucifixion.
Some people even laughed at him and were unkind to him while he was dying!
But during all this, Jesus never did anything to displease his Father.

They crucified him ... along with the criminals.
(Luke 23:33)

But why did Jesus have to do all this? That is a very good question.
Jesus did all these things for his people whom he loves.
Jesus knew that his little children could not be perfect,
so he was perfect for them! Then he died for them
so that God would not have to punish them
for the bad things they do.
Jesus took their place.
He was their **substitute**.

Christ died for our sins.
(1 Corinthians 15:3)

God was happy with Jesus and what he had done.
After Jesus' body had been in a grave for three days,
God raised him from the dead! This is called the resurrection.
Jesus showed himself to his disciples and then went back to his Father.
Even though he is now high in the heavens with God,
he never forgets his people that he was given.
He prays for them there and he always watches over them.

'He is not here; he has risen, just as he said.'
(Matthew 28:6)

Are you a gift for Jesus?

Do you want to belong to someone as kind and loving as he is?
Jesus has said that if you come to him, he will take even

you to be his very own! This is called salvation.
Ask Jesus to be your Savior today!

Jesus said, 'Let the little children come to me,
and do not hinder them ...'
(Matthew 19:14)

Did you ever want to be perfect? What would that be like?
You should be kind and good and helpful to everyone.
You would never lie or say mean words.
You would not even think bad thoughts.
Imagine if you were always obedient
(wouldn't your mum and dad be happy about that!).

You would always do what God's Bible told you to do
and you would never do anything it told you not to do.
In other words, you would never sin.

'... the Lord searches every heart and understands every desire and every thought.'
(1 Chronicles 28:9)

'Blessed ... are those who hear the word of God and obey it.'
(Luke 11:28)

But most of the time you really don't want to be perfect, do you?
When your big brother (or sister or mum or dad) makes you angry,
you want to say mean words, or hit. And it's hard to obey, isn't it?
You know you can't be perfect, not even for one day!

Did you know that God is perfect and fair and has to
punish every bad thing that is done?

Did you know that God's heaven is a perfect and clean place,
and only perfect people can go there? No sin is allowed.
Does this mean that you can never go to heaven?
No, it doesn't!

NO ONE UNDERSTANDS

HEARTBROKEN

ANGER

If we claim to be without sin, we deceive ourselves and the truth is not in us.
(1 John 1:8)

You are
HERE!

God sent his
son here
for YOU!

The Lord Jesus loves his people very much and he wants them to
come to heaven to be with him. That is why he came to earth.
He lived a perfect life for them and then died for them.
He was punished for their sins so that they
wouldn't have to be.

Jesus is the way to heaven!

So how can you get to heaven?
This is the most important question anyone will ever ask you.
Do you know the answer?
Jesus himself must change you.
If you're all dirty and smelly, you can't come in to eat dinner
without getting cleaned up and changing clothes.

Jesus must wash away all your filthy sin,
so that you can come into God's holy heaven.
He makes you clean, inside and out.

Jesus answered, 'I am the way and the truth and the life. No one comes to the Father except through me.'
(John 14:6)

Wash away all my iniquity and cleanse me from my sin.
(Psalm 51:2)

First, Jesus changes you on the inside. He sends the Holy Spirit
to give you a new spiritual heart that wants to be saved.
Regeneration is the big word for this.
But how do you know if you have a new heart?

Well, if you do, there are certain things that will happen.
The first thing your new heart will do is believe what the Bible says about Jesus.
Jesus did everything that had to be done for you to be saved.
He offers salvation as a gift!

'Believe in the Lord Jesus, and you will be saved ...'
(Acts 16:31)

This righteousness is given through faith in Jesus Christ to all who believe.
(Romans 3:22)

Did you pay your grandmother for the dolly or the truck that she gave you for your birthday? No, silly! Then it wouldn't be a gift.

You don't have to buy salvation by giving God money or even by being extra good. Your believing heart will take the gift of Jesus and what he did.

This is called having faith.

What is faith?

Faith is knowing that only Jesus can save you. Faith is telling him that you want this gift and that you want to be clean inside and outside.

But more than this, faith is your heart running to Jesus because there you will be safe. Your sin would keep you from God forever, but Jesus died for your sins and will forgive them.

God's little lambs run to the one Good Shepherd, the Lord Jesus; they rest in his strong arms and he carries them safely to heaven.

In Christ Jesus you are all children of God through faith.
(Galatians 3:26)

Do you want Jesus to be your Savior?
If you do, then you will be sorry for your sins,
the bad things you do.
This is called repentance.
Jesus hates sins.
He had to die so that God would forgive our sins.

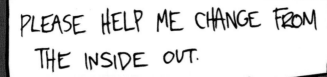

Little children who love and trust him are sad when they do wrong things. They hate sin and try to be good, because that pleases their Savior.

Faith and repentance are two signs of a new heart and a clean inside.

Jesus takes off your dirty smelly sin and dresses you in his own obedience to God.
When God looks at you, he forgives you.

He sees the nice clean obedience that Jesus has covered you with.
This is called justification.

'Repent ... and turn to God, so that your sins may be wiped out.'
(Acts 3:19)

Since we have been justified through faith,
we have peace with God through our Lord Jesus Christ.
(Romans 5:1)

Do you know anyone who is adopted?
When Jesus saves you, he makes you one of God's children.
He takes you into the family of God.
Isn't it exciting that God wants to be your heavenly Father?
This is the best family ever!

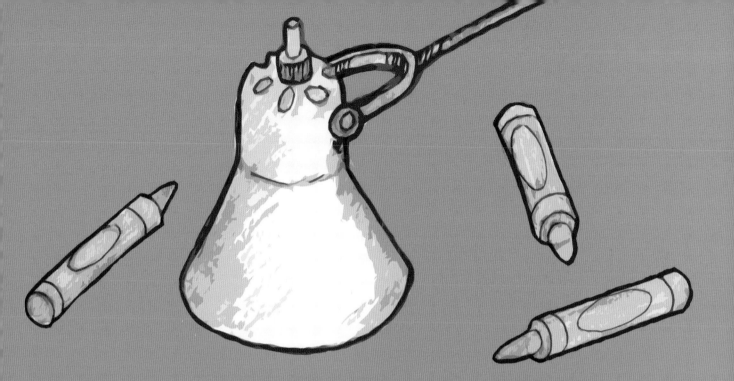

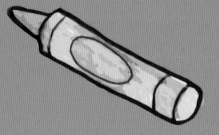

'I will be a Father to you,
and you will be my sons and daughters,
says the Lord Almighty.'

(2 Corinthians 6:18)

All these changes and great things that
God does for his children are called salvation.
Isn't salvation wonderful?

And there are even more blessings that God gives to you, if you are saved.
Jesus helps you more and more to turn from sin and to be good and
obedient and to please him. This is called sanctification. It lasts all your life.

And finally when you get to heaven, all the changes
will be finished. You will be perfect then!
(The Bible calls this last change glorification).

And you will sing songs to Jesus to thank him for saving you.

Thanks be to God for his indescribable gift!
(2 Corinthians 9:15)

'Everyone who calls on the name of the Lord will be saved.'
(Romans 10:13)

Has Jesus saved you?

If you're not sure, or you don't understand about salvation yet,
it is very important for you to find out more.
You and your family should find a church where you will worship God together.
You need to go to a church where you will hear God's preacher explain God's Word.

Ask all the questions you need to.
Read God's Bible or have someone read it to you.
Jesus loves little children.

Ask Jesus to change your heart today!